The Sons of Zebedee

A Biography of the Apostle James and John

By Matthew Murray

BookCaps™ Study Guides
www.bookcaps.com

© 2013. All Rights Reserved.

Cover Image © oxygen64 - Fotolia.com

Table of Contents

ABOUT LIFECAPS 4

INTRODUCTION 5

CHAPTER 1 7
- THE PROBLEM WITH COMMON NAMES 8
- HOMETOWN 10
- IDENTIFYING THEIR MOTHER 13

CHAPTER 2 17
- JESUS CALLS THE TWO BROTHERS TO DISCIPLESHIP 18
- THE CLUB OF THE INNER THREE 22
- POSSIBLE MYTHOLOGICAL ASSOCIATIONS 30
- PREFERENTIAL TREATMENT 33
- FIRE FROM HEAVEN 39

CHAPTER 3 42
- PETER AND JOHN 43
- THE ROGUE EXORCIST 47

CHAPTER 4 50
- FROM THE SYNOPTICS TO LATER LITERARY TRADITION 51
- THE JOURNEY FROM JERUSALEM TO EPHESUS ACCORDING TO THE ACTS OF JOHN 53
- THE JOURNEY FROM JERUSALEM TO EPHESUS ACCORDING TO THE CONTENDINGS OF THE APOSTLES 55
- JOHN'S ARRIVAL AT EPHESUS ACCORDING TO THE ACTS OF JOHN 59
- JOHN'S ARRIVAL AT EPHESUS ACCORDING TO THE CONTENDINGS OF THE APOSTLES 75
- JOHN AND THE TEMPLE OF ARTEMIS 82

CHAPTER 5 87
- JOHN AND THE PATRICIDAL MAN 88
- JOHN IN SMYRNA AND OTHER CITIES 93

John Returns to Ephesus 97
John and the Prodigal Ward 106
The Death of John 109

CHAPTER 6 111

A Biographical Sketch of the Writer of the Fourth Gospel ...112
The Epistles of John 117
The Book of Revelation 119

CHAPTER 7 121

James Travels to India 122
The Death of James 129

BIBLIOGRAPHY 131

About LifeCaps

LifeCaps is an imprint of BookCaps™ Study Guides. With each book, a lesser known or sometimes forgotten life is recapped. We publish a wide array of topics (from baseball and music to literature and philosophy), so check our growing catalogue regularly (**www.bookcaps.com**) to see our newest books.

Introduction

There were multiple cases when Jesus called disciples to himself, not individually, but as part of a wider family. Even when siblings and spouses were not officially included in the inner group of the twelve, there is evidence of their presence as disciples of Jesus in close proximity. James and John are probably the most well-known group of brothers because of their nickname, 'sons of thunder.' In addition, the tradition generally records a terrific deal of information about one family member and precious little about the other, apart from their familial relationship to their more famous family member. In the case of the brothers Simon Peter and Andrew, the gospel writers and the book of Acts make frequent mention of Simon Peter, who would become the 'rock' of the church. Andrew, his brother, on the other hand, is hardly mentioned apart from the preserved lists of the twelve. A similar situation holds with John and his brother James.

Chapter 1

The Problem with Common Names

Both John and James were common names in first century Palestine. The problem created by such common names is that when an ancient writer only mentions an individual by their given name, without any 'epithets', modifying phrases like the family (father's name) or the place of birth (origin) of the individual, it is difficult to know for certain which individual the ancient writer intends. In the case of the name John, in the Gospels and Acts alone there are at least four distinct individuals apart from the son of Zebedee who carried this name. There was John the Baptist, John the father of Simon Peter and Andrew (John 1:43; 21:15-17), John Mark

(Acts 12:12, 25; 13:5, 13; 15:37), and John the member of a high priestly family (Acts 4:6). In the case of the name James, one of the brothers of Jesus who also bore this name became one of the prominent leaders in the Jerusalem church after Jesus' death and resurrection. To avoid confusion between these two, James, the son of Zebedee, was nicknamed James the Less.

Hometown

James and John grew up in the region of Galilee, but the gospels never mention their hometown explicitly. Many New Testament scholars have taken the information supplied in the Fourth Gospel, that Peter, Andrew and Philip were from Bethsaida (John 1:44) and concluded that James and John were likely from Bethsaida, as well. This would seem to be little more than a guess.

While growing up, they would have spoken Aramaic. They may have attended a local synagogue while they were growing up, but they did not receive any formal religious training, which makes it unlikely that they knew Hebrew. Growing up in a small village in Galilee, there would have been no reason for them to learn Greek either. When they were old enough, they learned the fishing trade from their father, Zebedee. It is likely that they occasionally accompanied their father on his fishing boat even as young boys. Some early Christian traditions recorded that Zebedee was a priest. The prologue to the *Acts of John by Prochorus* states that Zebedee was a priest who lived in Jerusalem, near the temple (Culpepper, 1994, 61). There is also a statement by Polycrates, the Bishop of Ephesus (130-96 BCE), that John was a priest. The reason for this tradition is that the book of John makes reference to 'another disciple' who accompanied Peter into the courtyard of the high priest, because he was 'known to the high priest' (John 18:15). This identification relies on a long series of inferences. The set of inferences goes something like this: 1) the phrase 'another disciple' here refers to the 'Beloved Disciple'; 2) the 'Beloved Disciple' was John, the son of Zebedee; 3) in order for him to be known by the high priest, he must have been a priest himself; and 4) in order to be a priest himself, his father must have been a priest. Needless to say, this identification is quite flimsy at best.

Identifying their Mother

In the case of James and John, it is possible that the name of their mother was preserved in the New Testament for posterity, but this is still a conjecture. The conjecture depends upon lining up parallel passages from the gospel accounts. The relevant parallel involves the list of women who gathered at the foot of the cross during Jesus' crucifixion. The earliest gospel, Mark, records "There were also women looking on from a distance; among them were Mary Magdalene, and Mary the mother of James the younger and of Joses, and Salome. These used to follow him and provided for him when he was in Galilee…" (Mark 15:40-41, NRSV) The

Gospel of Mark both names these three women and goes on to clarify that they were all instrumental in Jesus' ministry activities in Galilee. The writer of the Gospel of Matthew words this passage slightly differently, where it appears "Many women were also there, looking on from a distance; they had followed Jesus from Galilee and had provided for him. Among them were Mary Magdalene, and Mary the mother of James and Joseph, and the mother of the sons of Zebedee." (Matt. 27:55-56). Here, only two of the women are named, whereas the third is identified by her sons. In Luke, the women at the foot of the cross are not named, but are lumped together under the heading "the women who had followed him from Galilee" (Luke 23:49, 55). The simplest solution is that the writer of Matthew substituted the phrase "the mother of the sons of Zebedee" for the name "Salome."

Such an equation would be without question,

were it not for the information contained in these gospels relating to the women who gathered at the tomb. In Mark, the same three women who appeared at the foot of the cross visit the tomb (Mark 16:1). In Matthew's gospel, only the two Mary's are present. Matthew does not mention the mother of the sons of Zebedee as he did earlier in the scene at the cross, or Salome, as his source Mark has it. Luke, meanwhile, who had left the women unnamed at the cross, names three women at the tomb—the two Mary's who have been mentioned by several other gospel writers and adds a new name, 'Joanna' (Luke 24:10). This means that using Mark, Luke substituted another woman entirely (Joanna), for Salome. The problem that this creates is that it raises the real possibility that Matthew was not simply substituting an epithet for a name referring to the same individual, but could have been substituting a different individual altogether (identified by an epithet).

Chapter 2

Jesus Calls the Two Brothers to Discipleship

According to Mark and Matthew, Jesus approached the brothers James and John while they were engaged in fishing related activities with their father. Their story is conflated with the similar story regarding the call of Simon (Peter) and his brother Andrew. It is helpful to consider the similarities and differences between the two sets of brothers and their respective calls.

Andrew and Simon are (presumably on shore) actually casting their nets into the sea. Jesus then issues his call to them to follow him promising to transform him from a fisher of fish, to a fisher of people. According to Mark, the fishermen do not engage in any type of clean up activity, but leave their nets where they are and follow Jesus.

James and John are specifically in their boat (or in their father's boat according to Matthew), mending their nets. Jesus sees them and issues his call for them to follow him. The two then leave their boat, their father and the hired men beside whom they were working and followed Jesus.

The Gospel of Luke is at marked variance with these traditional call narratives. It seems clear that Luke has taken a traditional post-resurrection story contained in the tradition (John 21:1-14) and co-opted it for the purposes of describing a call narrative (Luke 5:1-11). The reasons for this editorial change are not difficult to determine. For Luke geography was an integral part of how he told his story both in his gospel and in the sequel, the Book of Acts. In his gospel, Luke moves from describing Jesus' ministry in Galilee to his journey to Jerusalem, to the Passion and resurrection, which culminates in a mission beginning from Jerusalem that then expands in concentric circles in the Book of Acts. In Luke's geographical scheme, there is no place for a Galilean appearance in a post-resurrection setting. Therefore, Luke transformed the story into one related to the call of the fisherman.

In this story, Jesus is teaching the people along the shore when they begin to crowd him. He then climbs into the boat belonging to Peter and asks Peter to take him out a little ways into the lake so that he can address the crowds. Jesus then sits down in the boat and addresses the crowd gathered on the shoreline. Once he has finished speaking, he asks Simon to cast his net into the water to catch some fish. Peter begins to argue with him that they have been struggling all night long to catch some fish and have been unable to do so. Jesus tells him to go ahead and do it anyway, and Peter pulls in a catch large enough to rip his nets. When Peter realizes that he is in trouble and will need some help with the haul, he summons Jams and John, who are his partners to help him. The final catch is so large that it threatens to sink both boats. As the fisherman are standing flabbergasted at the size of the catch, Jesus then issues his call to Peter declaring that he will transform him into a fisher of people. All four fishermen, Peter, Andrew, James and John then leave their boats to follow Jesus.

The Club of the Inner Three

Paul's letters constitute by far the earliest stratum of information concerning the early church. When information appears in these letters concerning the early church it is always given precedence over any information contained in the gospels or the Book of Acts. In Paul's letter to the churches in Galatia, several Jewish Christians from Jerusalem have arrived in Galatia and are attempting to undermine Paul's authority. In an effort to reestablish his authority with the community, he summarizes his conversion story and his commission to preach the gospel to the Gentiles (including those in Galatia) (Gal. 1:11-2:10). One of the points that he makes is that he, along with Barnabus and Titus, visited Jerusalem, where the three pillars (leaders) of the church, James, Cephas (Peter) and John gave their blessing for the Gentile mission (Gal. 2:1-10). The James in this context is James, the brother of Jesus, not James, the brother of John. In any case, it is probably not a coincidence that the inner circle of three described in the Gospel of Mark is a group with the same names as these early 'pillars.'

In the Gospel of Mark, the three disciples, Peter, James and John stand apart from the other nine disciples. In the first place, Jesus gives each of them a specific name apart from their given name. Simon is given the Greek name Peter, which becomes the name by which this disciple is known. James and John receive a name that applies to them as brothers, *Boanerges* (Mark 3:17). Mark explains that Jesus named Simon, Peter, because "upon this rock I will build my church" (Mark 16:18). New Testament scholars have little trouble explaining this reference, because the Greek word for rock is *petros*, which is identical with the way the name Peter appears in Greek. The name *Boanerges,* on the other hand, is a different matter altogether. Mark provides a gloss to this name as 'sons of thunder' (Mark 3:17). But the Hebrew or Aramaic word(s) to which this title refers remains a mystery some two thousand years later.

There are at least five different Hebrew/Aramaic words that would fit this Greek transliteration, but the one that actually means 'thunder' would correspond to *Boanergem*, not *Boanerges*. There is one word meaning 'commotion,' another meaning 'anger,' and a third meaning 'earthquake' that have all been proposed as possibilities. Even the first part of the title, one of the most common words in Hebrew/Aramaic, does not fit the well with the usual Hebrew/Aramaic word meaning 'sons', *bne*. The vowel between the /b/ and the /n/ in both languages is a short indistinct vowel. The question of how such a short vowel came to be represented by the sequence *omicron-alpha* in Greek has tormented scholars.

But even on a more basic level, assuming that a Hebrew/Aramaic equivalent to 'sons of thunder' could be authoritatively produced, what does it mean? Some scholars have argued that it refers to their being hot-tempered. Others have regarded it as a reference to their role as zealots (not otherwise attested). One scholar suggests that the original Hebrew/Aramaic term has modified slightly (note the strange vowel change mentioned above) to match a Greek term, meaning 'shout-workers,' which would translate idiomatically into 'loud-mouths.' Unlike the name change with Simon Peter, Jesus provides no explanation for the name in the tradition.

In addition to the name, in Mark's gospel, there are three different incidents where Jesus singles out these three disciples from the rest to accompany him; the raising of Jairus' daughter; the transfiguration; and the Garden of Gethsemane. There is also a fourth scene where this inner group expands to four members, the Olivet Discourse. This singling out of a group of inner disciples within the standard group of twelve is consistent with Mark's overarching theme of the Messianic secret. The raising of Jairus' daughter is the only resurrection miracle that appears in the Gospel of Mark.

In the story in Mark, Peter, James and John accompany Jesus to Jairus' house. Once they are there, Jesus invites only these three disciples and the child's parents into the room where he is to perform the miracle. Thus, in Mark, only these three disciples are privy to Jesus' power to raise people from the dead and Jesus orders them to keep what they have seen a secret.

Similarly, in the scene of the transfiguration, Peter, James and John receive an invitation from Jesus to accompany him up the mountain. These three then see a vision of Jesus glowing as an angelic figure and joined by Elijah and Moses. They also here a voice from heaven declaring Jesus to be the 'Son of God.' Here again, as they descend the mountain Jesus asks them to keep what they saw a secret.

The next two scenes differ slightly from the pattern of the first two in that they do not contain the admonition to keep what they have seen or heard a secret. In place of this order to remain silent is an order to "Keep awake." The third scene is the Olivet Discourse (a sermon or set of lessons delivered on the Mount of Olives) where a fourth member appears with the inner group of three—Peter's brother, Andrew. After Jesus has taken these four disciples aside, he provides a fantastic deal of apocalyptic information about the signs and portents relating to the end of the world. Unlike the previous two scenes, this sermon contains no statements indicating that Jesus is the 'Son of God' so there is no need for the admonitions to secrecy. Instead, Jesus encourages the four disciples to be vigilant regarding what he has shared with them.

In the Garden of Gethsemane, the scene returns to Jesus only inviting these select three disciples to join him. In this case, there is actually no special revelation to the three. Jesus does, however, ask them to stay awake as he had done at the Mount of Olives. The situation in this case, though, is less metaphorical, and Jesus literally wants them to stay awake at this late hour. They fail to do so twice and Jesus chastises them for it, specifically singling out Peter as the recipient of his rebuke.

Possible Mythological Associations

Derrett has argued that the Christian tradition regarding James and John that stands behind the Synoptic Gospels associated them with the famous twins from Greek mythology Castor and Pollux, the Dioscuri. To make this connection, he notes six general characteristics of the Greek twins: they were identified with the stars; they were helpers in distress; they were champions on horseback; they were saviors from shipwreck; they were interested in hospitality; and they were averters of evil omens (Derrett, 1980, 301-2). Derrett then draws connections between these literary motifs and the subjects about which Jesus chooses to converse with James and

John in the Olivet Discourse. Jesus talks with the brothers about the stars (Mark 13:24-27, 31-32); the times of day, connected with the evening and morning stars (Mark 13:33-37); the weather (13:17-18); the seasons (13:28-29); earthquakes, famines, troubles and sorrows (13:8, 19-20); war (13:7); and rescue from danger (13:13-16). Initially reading his list sounds quite compelling.

But stepping back, it is clear that these are not subjects of discourse addressed to James and John scattered throughout the book of Mark, but subjects that are culled from one particular chapter with apocalyptic themes where the subjects of war and heavenly bodies are the expected themes. Moreover, the address in Mark 13 is not specifically to James and John, but also includes Peter and his brother Andrew. With such a perspective, there seems to be little connection between Castor and Pollux as represented in Greek mythology and the apostles James and John.

Preferential Treatment

Besides their call narrative, there are a few stories contained in the gospel accounts that describe events that took place involving these two brothers. As with many stories relating to the disciples, most of these stories do not paint the brothers in a positive light. In the Gospel of Mark, the two brothers ask a rather impertinent question of Jesus. As if they had found in Jesus a genie-in-a-bottle, they ask him to grant them a wish of whatever their heart desires. In a much more tactful manner, Jesus inquires further as to what that wish might be. The brothers clarify that they would like to be seated on either side of Jesus in his coming kingdom (in glory).

Before moving on to Jesus' reply, the hubris in this request almost strains credulity even for the disciples. It is one thing for them to be arguing amongst themselves as to who is 'top dog' in the group, but to make such a request of their teacher and master seems crass indeed. In the Gospel of Matthew, it is not the disciples themselves, but rather their mother, who makes the request of Jesus. Such a situation sounds far more plausible historically speaking. The tradition is clear that their mother followed Jesus and his disciples closely, and while this question would be ludicrous for the brothers to ask for themselves, it sounds like just the sort of thing that a mother would ask for her children.

But there are two strong reasons for supposing that the Matthean tradition where their mother asks the question is actually secondary. While English does not make a distinction between second person singular 'you' and second person plural 'you,' Greek does make this distinction. In the dialogue as it is narrated in Matthew, it is the mother of James and John who asks Jesus the question, but Jesus' subsequent dialogue is entirely with the two brothers and does not acknowledge their mother at all. Another point that is relevant here is that there is a way to interpret this question that sounds much more reasonable and realistic. Lane raised the possibility that given the tradition of the circle of the inner three and several comments in John's gospel, it is possible that this was the seating arrangement when the twelve disciples ate meals with Jesus, with John on Jesus' right hand side and James on Jesus' left hand side. The question of the brothers, then went something like, since we have established this seating order during your time here on earth, will that same seating order be maintained in your heavenly kingdom.

When phrased in this context, the question no longer seems to come out of left field and makes sense coming directly from the brothers. Returning to the dialogue itself, Jesus rebukes the two brothers indicating their continued ignorance. There is then a further difference between the two accounts. In the Markan version, he asks them two follow up questions, relating to the cup and baptism. The coupling of these two images cannot fail to conjure images of the early Christian sacraments of the Eucharist (communion) and baptism, which as practiced in the early church both signified Jesus' death. The arrangement in Matthew again seems more consistent with the scene in the life of Jesus, where the cup is often used throughout the Old Testament as a symbol for suffering (see Ps. 11:6 and Is. 51:17).

So Jesus asks the brothers if they are able to drink from the cup from which he will (soon) drink. The implied answer to his question (or to both of his questions) is 'no' they cannot suffer what Jesus is about to suffer. But in a kind of comical sit-com-like interchange, the brothers reply with an affirmative answer. They say of course we can pick up the (physical) cup that you will pick up (at dinner) and drink from it, and presumably they too (along with the other disciples) received the baptism of John the Baptist along with Jesus. In the Markan version, when Jesus confirms that they have answered correctly, the reader hears it as a confirmation of the practice of the sacraments in which the early church will engage. In the version in Matthew, it is as if he acknowledges that they will suffer a similar fate as Jesus. One problem with this interpretation is that while the martyrdom of James is recorded in Acts 12:2, there is no consistent tradition indicating that John was martyred, and the most prominent account of his death was a peaceful ordeal. Jesus then goes on to explain that he does not have the authority to grant the request they (or their mother) have asked of him, but that such authority lies with his heavenly Father.

Fire From Heaven

The Gospel of Luke alone contains one story where the two brothers, James and John, speak alone to Jesus. In the narrative context of Luke, Jesus is on his way from Galilee to Jerusalem for the Passover festival. Along the way, Jesus dispatches messengers charged with finding suitable lodging and accommodations for he and his disciples. The messengers return from a Samaritan village indicating that although there would otherwise be vacancy, the innkeepers will not put them up for the night because they are travelling to celebrate a religious festival in Jerusalem and their was much animosity between the religious practices of the two groups. It is unclear whether the innkeepers themselves were being inhospitable, or whether they simply feared reprisals and problems from the other townspeople with which they did not want to deal. In either case, it was clear from the messengers that there was strong animosity towards them from members of that village.

It is at this point that James and John step into the spotlight, asking Jesus whether he would like them to call down fire from heaven upon the village in order to destroy it. This request has literary reverberations with the story of Elijah in 2 Kings who calls down fire from heaven to consume the prophets of Baal. But Luke takes pain to draw both parallels and divergences between the ministry of Jesus and that of Elijah. This is clearly one of the cases of divergence. Unlike Elijah, Jesus rebukes the two brothers for their request. The best manuscripts simply state that Jesus rebuked them and do not elaborate (Luke 5:54-56). But multiple later manuscripts elaborate upon the rebuke as follows "You do not know of whose spirit you are, for the Son of Man has not come to destroy peoples lives, but to save them" (Metzger, 1975, 148-49).

Several scholars have tried to make a connection between this story and the name that Jesus gave to these two brothers. The problem with this assertion is that unlike Mark, Luke nowhere mentions *Boanerges*. While it is possible that the story that led to their nickname became disconnected from the name itself, this seems like idle scholarly speculation with little support.

Chapter 3

Peter and John

In addition to traditions that describe both brothers acting together, there are several passages that describe John acting apart from James. In some of these instances, John is not alone, but he and Peter seem to form an even tighter inner circle within the inner circle of three. This tradition appears in the Gospel of Luke and in its sequel, the Book of Acts and also appears in the Book of John.

The first scene that these two act as a pair is in the preparations for the Passover meal in Jerusalem. In the book of Mark, two unnamed disciples travel to make preparations for the

Passover meal (Mark 14:13). In Luke's retelling of the story, he identifies the two disciples as Peter and John (Luke 22:8). It seems odd that if the identities of these two disciples were common knowledge in the tradition that the author of Mark would have left such information out of the narrative. On the other hand, it would make sense for Luke to seize on the opportunity afforded by the anonymity of the two disciples in this scene to introduce Peter and John as a pair that would pave the way for readers to be accustomed to the pairing when they got to the Book of Acts.

But if we assume that the Beloved Disciple was John, the son of Zebedee, then the book of John pairs these two up on several occasions. At the Last Supper, when Jesus reveals to the disciples that one among them will betray him, Peter gives the old head nod to the Beloved Disciple, who is leaning on Jesus and asks him to ask Jesus to identify the betrayer (John 13:21-24). Also, when the disciples learn from the women that Jesus is no longer in the tomb, some of them run to the tomb to see for themselves. In the Gospel of Luke, only Peter is named, but at another point Luke acknowledges that those who went to check on the tomb included more than just Peter (Luke 24:12, 24). In the Gospel of John, Peter and the Beloved Disciple get into an all out foot race to the tomb, with the Beloved Disciple beating Peter there (John 20:3-10).

In the Book of Acts, the pairing of Peter and John is unmistakable. Nevertheless, whenever John appears alongside Peter it is only the latter who speaks. Peter and John travel together to the Jerusalem temple for prayer when a crippled man stops hem asking for alms (Acts 3:1-10). On another occasion, both Peter and John are preaching to the people in Jerusalem, and the authorities arrest both of them (Acts 4:1-22). When they are released, both of them say a prayer together in the hearing of the people. A third scene involves a joint missionary effort to Samaria. The two traveled together to the region and laid hands on the new group of believers so that they might receive the Holy Spirit (Acts 8:14-25). The group had been baptized, but had not yet learned of the Holy Spirit. The two then return to Jerusalem together. It seems clear from these scenes that Peter and John were prominent leaders in the early Jerusalem church and that the author of Luke-Acts wanted to convey that to his audience.

The Rogue Exorcist

In addition to singling out the inner three, Mark contains one story (repeated by Luke) that features John as the spokesman for the entire group of disciples. Given the fact that Peter tends to be the spokesman for the group in most other instances, this story is probably the best reflection of the character of John. Although there has been some argument as to whether this scene ultimately goes back to Jesus or whether it reflects a later concern of the early church, the liberal answer that Jesus gives argues strongly in favor of a historical story that can be traced back to Jesus himself even by the harshest of historical critics.

The story falls immediately after the disciples have been bickering among themselves who is the greatest and Jesus brings a little child beside him as a visual reminder about the inverted nature of the social stratification in his kingdom. It is immediately following this scene that John speaks up and mentions that they saw a man who was not a follower of Jesus casting out demons using the exorcism formula that he had taught them, which involved invoking Jesus' name. John noted that he and the other disciples tried to stop this individual from what he was doing. Jesus then rebukes John for the question seeing no problem in someone else co-opting his exorcism formula. Jesus then takes the common phrase, "whoever is not for us is against us" and turns it on its head, saying, "whoever is not against us is for us" (Mark 9:40).

One of the most interesting takeaways from this story is that it provides the most compelling argument against identifying John, the son of

Zebedee, with the author of the Fourth Gospel. This story suggests that John had a strong interest in exorcism, whereas the Fourth Gospel fails to mention even one of Jesus' exorcisms.

Chapter 4

From the Synoptics to Later Literary Tradition

When moving away from the Synoptic Gospels, the picture of John the son of Zebedee, becomes more complex. The Johannine literature, which is the term New Testament scholars use to refer to the Gospel of John, the Epistles of John and the book of Revelations, has been attributed to John, the son of Zebedee, from very early in the history of the church. In order to do this, the tradition describes a narrative of the life of John, the son of Zebedee, after Jesus' death and resurrection that connects him as the author of all three of these subsequent Johannine sources.

The Journey from Jerusalem to Ephesus according to the Acts of John

The *Acts of John* is a second century compilation that tells the following account of John's life after Pentecost (Schäferdiek, 2003, 152-209). John had a vision one night wherein the Lord told him to go to Ephesus. He then packed up his belongings leaving his Galilean home and headed for Ephesus. While he was travelling to Ephesus, a member of his family (Aristodemus) and two of his friends (Demonicus and Cleobius) managed after much cajoling to persuade John to stop for one day in Miletus, a town about 25 miles south of Ephesus on the coast of the Aegean Sea. While he was visiting with them, the Lord spoke from heaven a word of blessing and prophecy concerning the work he was to carry out in Ephesus. His companions heard the voice and rejoiced greatly with him. The four of them then headed together on to Ephesus.

The Journey from Jerusalem to Ephesus according to the Contendings of the Apostles

The *Contendings of the Apostles* is an Ethiopic text most likely composed around the sixth century CE. According to this account, John travelled with Prochorus from Jerusalem to Joppa. Once at Joppa, they boarded a ship headed for Asia on their way to Ephesus. When they were onboard, John had a premonition that something bad would happen to him during the journey. He, therefore, pulled Prochorus aside and asked him that whatever should happen, he was to make his way to Ephesus and wait there for two months. If he did not die and was able,

John would make his way to Ephesus and meet Prochorus there. If Prochorus did not see him after two months, he should return to Jerusalem and find James, the brother of Jesus, and take further instructions from him. Later that day, the winds and waves picked up and battered the ship violently. The ship finally broke into pieces, and all of the crew clung to the debris that remained floating in the sea. All of the merchandize and money that they carried on board was lost at sea. The tide then carried the survivors to Seleucia, where every one aboard the ship washed up with the exception of John. When the crewmembers finally regained their strength and were able to talk again, they developed a conspiracy theory that someone had sabotaged the ship in order to steal off with the money and merchandise aboard the ship. Since John was the only person onboard the ship who did not wash up on shore with the rest of the crew, they deduced that he was the mastermind behind the plot.

They grabbed Prochorus and accused him of being an accomplice in the plot since he and John had been travelling together. They dragged him before the leaders of the city who sided with the crewmembers since they outnumbered Prochorus by a large margin. They put Prochorus in prison and accused John of sorcery. They interrogated Prochorus mercilessly, but he only replied that he was a Christian from Judah travelling as a missionary to Ephesus. An officer from Antioch arrived and persuaded the officials to let Prochorus go.

Prochorus then travelled for forty days on his way to Ephesus. He stopped at a village on the coast named Mareon where he sat down to rest and sleep. When he awoke, he saw a man's body wash up on the shore. He ran to the spot where the man was and help drag him out of the sea and further onto the shore. When he got a good look at the man, he realized it was John and was overcome with joy. They hugged and cried and thanked God together that they had met up at last. As soon as John had time to catch his breath, he explained to Prochorus that he had spend the past forty days and nights in the depths of the sea. The two then slowly made there way from Mareon to Ephesus.

John's Arrival at Ephesus according to the Acts of John

No sooner had John begun to enter the city gate of Ephesus, than a wealthy man named Lycomedes stopped him informing him of the plight of his wife, who had become paralyzed over the course of the last week. Lycomedes described the dire situation and pled with John to come and heal his wife. He explained to John that the Lord had appeared to him in a dream, reassuring him from his fear and informing him that someone named John would be coming from Miletus who would be able to heal his wife, Cleopatra. Therefore, he asked that John would come quickly since his wife could now make no further movement than simply breathing. John and his companions quickly followed the man to his house, only a short distance from the city gate.

As soon as they entered the house, Lycomedes became filled with grief and began to lament over his beautiful young wife, Cleopatra. He wailed and cried out that all was lost and that his virtuous and righteous life had been wasted. He declared that he would kill himself before she died so that he might then stand before Lady Justice and indict her for punishing Cleopatra unjustly. When Lycomedes had concluded his mad raving, John grabbed him by the shoulders to shake some sense into the man. He berated him for not having trusted the Lord who had appeared to him in a vision. He asked Lycomedes instead to stand and pray to the Lord for the health of his wife and to believe that he would not lose her. But instead of standing and praying, Lycomedes fell to the floor first lamenting, then motionless, as if he were dead.

This immensely frustrated John, who had come to this house to heal a woman and now, as far as he could tell, was surrounded by two dead bodies—hardly the sign of a miracle-worker. The crowd, who was growing larger by the minute, standing outside would now judge him a fraud and cast him out of the city in sharp contradiction to the vision he had received earlier that day. John then prayed that God would raise up the man and his wife, who now lay dead in their own house. As the crowd outside continued to swell, he continued praying both that he would not be defamed in front of the Ephesians to whom he desired to minister and that they would come to faith as a result of the miraculous healing he was asking Jesus to perform. Once he concluded his long, fervent prayer, John then walked over to Cleopatra, who was lying lifeless on the bed and spoke a resurrection formula over her. The formula had its desired effect and she sat up after having been paralyzed for seven days to the amazement of the assembled crowd.

John then calmly addressed Cleopatra asking her not to be alarmed as he related that her husband Lycomedes lie dead in the adjoining room. He asked her to have faith and assured her that he would raise her husband back to life, just as he had done with her. She braced herself as the two entered the bedroom, but upon seeing her husband, she lost her voice, ground her teeth, and bit her tongue as tears ran down her face. When John saw the way that Cleopatra restrained herself despite the utter grief that was welling up within her, he decided to allow her to pronounce the formula over her husband herself. He prayed briefly with her and explained why he thought she should do this; then he provided her with the resurrection formula. She walked up to the couch on which he was lying and uttered the formula that John had taught her. At once, Lycomedes stood up and then seeing John, fell down before him kissing his feet. But John chastised Lycomedes gently telling him that he should not be kissing his feet, but rather the feet of God who raised him from the dead. The couple then pled with John to stay with them while he remained in the city. John wanted to only stay for one night, but his companions persuaded him that they should stay with the couple, and John relented.

Lycomedes was so grateful to John for having saved his life and the life of his wife that he began to revere the Apostle and to honor him as if he were a god. Having used various idols and images as a means to worship all his life, Lycomedes got an idea. A friend of his was a skilled painter. He would ask his friend to paint a portrait of John that he might be ever reminded of the one who saved the lives of him and his wife. As soon as he conceived the plan he ran to his friend and asked him for the favor.

Lycomedes knew, however, that John would not approve of the portrait. Therefore, he asked his friend if he would be able to make the portrait while concealing himself from the Apostle. His friend indicated it would be no trouble at all and made the sketch and outline on the first day and colored it in appropriately on the second.

Lycomedes was so pleased to have this portrait of John, and he hung it in his bedroom hanging garlands around it and setting up an altar before it. As John was still living in their house, Lycomedes continued to be careful not to let John see the portrait. John picked up on his strange behavior and thinking that his friend was masturbating called him on it. "My dear child, what is it you are doing when you come from the bath into your bedroom alone?" (Acts of John 27) Embarrassed, Lycomedes led John into his bedroom. Now John had never before seen his own reflection before. When he saw the portrait of some old man and the altar and garlands surrounding it, he concluded that this must be one of Lycomedes' pagan gods. Lycomedes reiterated that he now only worshipped the one true God who had raised him from the dead. But he went on to explain that he also honors and venerates John for having guided him to the living God and that he had this portrait made of him.

John began to laugh out loud saying, "Come on, you are just pulling my leg. There is no way that old man in the portrait is a likeness of me." Lycomedes then turned around and retrieved a mirror from a table in his bedroom and held it up before John's face. John was aghast to realize how old and decrepit he now looked. John then took the opportunity to preach to Lycomedes and talked at length about how this portrait only captures the image of him in the flesh. No doubt John believed that his soul and spirit were much more comely in form than this awful picture he had just seen. He then made an analogy between different color paints and the virtues of the Christian life and encouraged Lycomedes to 'paint' with these virtues.

While he was staying in Ephesus with Lycomedes and Cleopatra, John obtained an assistant named Verus, who was one of the members of the newly formed church. John sent Verus throughout Ephesus to gather all the women over the age of sixty so that John, Lycomedes and Cleopatra could care for them. Verus reported back that as he traversed the city he was able to find only four elderly women who were in good physical health. The rest of the women he found were either: paralyzed, deaf, arthritic or beset with various other debilitating diseases. For John, these bodily symptoms were not simply the result of old age taking its toll on these women, but rather, reflected an inner spiritual condition that permeated the city. Throughout the following day, Verus brought a few women at a time to Lycomedes' house where John instructed them to meet him the following day in the theater to await their healing.

The following day the theater was packed before the sun came up. The governmental leaders of Ephesus heard about this spectacle, and many came to the theater to see for themselves what would take place. One leader in particular, Andronicus, challenged John through the rumor mill to perform his miracle with these old women with two stipulations: 1) he was to appear naked in the theater so that the crowd would know he had nothing up his sleeve; and 2) he was to not pronounce the 'magical' name that he is reported to pronounce. When news of the challenge reached John, he was greatly disturbed by it.

Nevertheless, he instructed the women to enter the theater as he took center stage. With such a vast audience assembled, John took the opportunity to preach the gospel of Jesus Christ to them all. Unfortunately, there is a large chunk of the manuscript upon which this story was preserved that is missing so it cuts off in the middle of his sermon. From various tidbits of information provided later in the story, scholars have reconstructed the plot of the missing section in the following way.

John heals the diseases and afflictions of all the old women, who were brought before him in the theater. The crowd was astounded at the sight, and many in the crowd believed in Jesus, as a result, including the wife of John's detractor, Andronicus, whose name was Drusiana. As a result of her conversion and John's preaching, Drusiana took a vow of chastity and would no longer sleep with her husband. This drove her husband crazy. As far as he was concerned, not only had John corrupted her with this new religion, now she denied him his conjugal rights. In a rage, he shut Drusiana up in a sepulcher attempting to force her into renouncing her vow. When she still refuses he leaves her there to die.

He then tracks down John and has him arrested and imprisoned, where Andronicus tries to starve him to death. The risen Christ appears to Drusiana, and she is miraculously saved from certain peril. Perhaps an earthquake or some other miraculous phenomenon saves John from his fate in the prison cell, as well. When he sees his plot foiled by God himself, Andronicus repents of his sin, converts to Christianity and joins his wife Drusiana in her vow of chastity.

The story then picks up again after the damaged section with Drusiana relating her experience of the risen Christ while she lay trapped in the tomb. She explained that first she saw the Lord appear as the Apostle John and then she saw him appear as a young man. The congregation who was gathered listening to Drusiana's story were confused by the theological implications that it conveyed. John saw their confusion and provided his own theological explanation for Drusiana's experience. The way John explained it, he had attained spiritual insight during his time with Jesus that was too profound for these new believers to understand. Therefore, he adapted himself and his teaching to make it understandable for them at their current level of spiritual maturity. John explained that Jesus behaves in a similar fashion.

For instance, when Jesus called he and his brother James, James saw a child standing on the shore summoning them, whereas John saw a grown man. When his brother described what he saw, John joked with him that he must be hallucinating from the long day of hard work out on the water. They both agreed to follow the figure to solve the riddle of who was seeing things. As they followed Jesus further inland, John then saw him as a bald-headed man with a long, thick beard, whereas now his brother, James, described seeing a young man with a beard just forming as opposed to the child he had seen earlier. John went on to explain that

Jesus continued to change in appearance as they spent time with him. John would stare at him for long periods never once seeing him blink or close his eyes to rest them. He occasionally appeared ugly, continually looking up into heaven.

His looks were not the only physical change that John noticed. Making reference to the descriptions of the Beloved Disciple in the Gospel of John, John described that as they lounged around the dinner table, he would lean his head against Jesus' chest. Sometimes his chest felt soft and smooth, while, at other times, it was hard as a rock. John then proceeded to describe the transfiguration, where Peter, his brother James and himself saw light emanating from Jesus that was unlike that of any mortal. He also described the time that they prayed with Jesus in the Garden of Gethsemane. He explained that he crept up to Jesus while he was kneeling in prayer and was astonished to realize that he was looking at his bare backside. His feet were white and lit up the ground around them. His head then stretched all the way up to heaven. John explained that he screamed when he saw the sight, which disturbed Jesus from his prayer. Jesus then turned around and grabbed John by his beard and reproved him for not having faith. John's face and jaw hurt so badly that he couldn't help but ask Jesus, if this is how bad it hurts when you simply grab me by the beard, I can't imagine what kind of pain I would be in were you to have backhanded me. Jesus' reply was something to the effect of, "Don't worry about that—just make sure it doesn't happen again."

John went on to describe that when he would reach out to pat Jesus on the back or to grasp his shoulder, sometimes he would touch him like an ordinary man, while at other times, his hand would pass right through Jesus as if through a ghost. He also would try to look to determine whether Jesus left footprints, because he often noticed that Jesus would levitate slightly, not even touching the earth.

He relates that on occasions when they would be invited to dine at the house of a Pharisee, that each one of the twelve disciples would be given a loaf of bread to eat with their meal and Jesus, as well. But on these occasions, Jesus would break his loaf up and begin to distribute it among the disciples. His disciples in turn, including John, would set down their own loaves only eating from Jesus' loaf until each was full. These miracles would astound the Pharisees with whom they dined.

John then turned from making the point by Jesus' physical appearance and attributes, to referencing Jesus' teaching itself. Along this line, John taught the congregation a long hymn that he was taught by Jesus shortly before his arrest. This hymn (portions of which are also coincidently cited by Augustine) is filled with paradoxes that serve to reinforce John's point that Jesus appears in many guises. After singing the hymn with his congregation, John then describes how Jesus then led him away and showed him a Cross of Light. Here again, John makes his point when Jesus lists some fifteen or twenty different names that the cross may go by. John then concludes his explanation by exhorting his congregation to worship the unchangeable God.

John's Arrival at Ephesus according to the Contendings of the Apostles

The Ethiopic text of the *Contendings of the Apostles* relates a quite different tale of what became of John when he came to Ephesus. John and Prochorus went up to the bathhouse in Ephesus, which was owned by the governor, Dioscorides. John told Prochorus that they should keep their identity a secret for some time in this new city. They were then met by the keeper of the bath, Romna. She was one ugly sight to behold. She was fat and strong and had no problem with beating those under her charge. Romna recognized them at once as being wanderers, new to the city, so she offered them both jobs. She offered John the job of stoking the fire in the bath and Prochorus the job of washing the bath. She paid them three loaves of bread for four days worth of work.

Now John had never before worked at stoking a fire so he was not good at the job when he started. Romna beat him mercilessly for his incompetence and laziness. Prochorus was sorry to see John treated so harshly, but John reassured him that this lot was better than being in the sea for forty days. After a few weeks, the keeper of the bath became quite agitated that John did not perform his task up to her expectations. He tried to explain to Romna that he had never performed such work before and that it was not because he was lazy, but because the work involved a learning curve. Romna would have none of it and began to drive the two out of her employ in a rage. But then another idea dawned on her, and she asked them to admit that they were her slaves. John replied stolidly that he was the fireman and Prochorus the washer of her bathhouse.

She then went to her lover, who was one of the officers of the governor and explained to him that she had two slaves who had run away from her and her parents many years ago. These two slaves had only recently returned. She asked her lover if he would be willing to write a slave deed for her declaring that these two were her slaves. The officer agreed that he would write a contract up for her as long as they acknowledged n his presence that they were her father's slaves. Romna then found the two of them in the bathhouse and rebuked them for not anticipating her arrival. She then dragged them before the temple and three witnesses and had a slave contract for them drawn up.

The story goes on to describe that this bathhouse was actually haunted. It had been built over a young girl who was still alive and her spirit continued to haunt the bathhouse killing one person on three set days each year. The governor, Dioscorides, knew that the place was haunted when he purchased it, and was careful to ensure that neither he nor his handsome son, Domos visited the bathhouse on those set days when the spirit took a life. One day, after John and Prochorus had been working there for about three months, the Dioscorides was preoccupied with city business, and Domos entered the bath alone, not knowing that this was one of the days the spirit took her vengeance in the bathhouse. The young man entered the bath and no sooner had he done so than the spirit took his life. The servants found Domos dead in the bath and cried out for grief explaining the situation to the keeper of the bath. Romna was overcome with fear, sure that her boss would kill her when he discovered that his son had died. She turned to Artemis, the city goddess of Ephesus, and began tearing out her hair in clumps appealing to the goddess for help.

Romna then returned to the bath finding John conversing with Prochorus. She then let all her frustration out on John in a series of vitriolic insults. John did not try to defend himself against her words, but simply walked into the bathhouse where he found Domos. He then cast out the demon from the boy, bringing him back to life again. John then presented the boy alive to the keeper of the bath acknowledging that he was brought back to life by the power of Jesus Christ. When Romna saw this, she was overcome with remorse repenting for how she had treated John from falsely enslaving him to the beatings and verbal abuse that she had heaped upon him. When he saw her repentance, he made the sign of the cross on her and she became a follower of Christ.

While he was still speaking with his employer and Domos, a servant of Dioscorides entered in a panic explaining that he had brought the news of Domos' death straightaway to Dioscorides as soon as he learned of it and that the shock of the news caused Dioscorides to faint and die. Domos ran to his father and found him dead, just as the servant had described. He then ran back to the bathhouse and pleaded with John to come and restore his father to life just as he had done for him. John reassured Domos that he would grant his request and the four of them walked to where Dioscorides lay followed by a large crowd of onlookers. John then uttered the resurrection formula and Dioscrorides rejoined the land of the living. Dioscorides then began to worship John as a God. But John was quick to correct him, and used the opportunity to preach the gospel to him and to the gathered crowd.

Romna then brought to John the slave contract that she had drawn up on his behalf. He tore the paper up in the presence of the people. He then reentered the bathhouse and cast out the spirit of the dead girl who had been haunting the bathhouse for years.

John and the Temple of Artemis

Another episode related both in the *Acts of John* and in the *Contendings of the Apostles* occurs when John suggests that he and his companions from Miletus visit the temple of Artemis before moving on to Smyrna. The city was holding a dedication festival for their goddess, and the entire city turned out adorned in white for the festive occasion. John took the opportunity instead to mourn the occasion and dressed all in black. Several of the people became incensed by his clothing and grabbed for him trying to kill him. But John managed to make his way to the podium and addressed the crowd. He rebuked the city for their unbelief despite the many miracles that he had performed in his short time there. He then offered them a bold challenge. He asked them to pray to their goddess Artemis and entreat his death. John, in turn, would pray to his God for the death of all of them.

Having seen the miracles that John performed, the people of the city were terrified by this prospect. They pleaded for mercy from him and acknowledged that they believed he could kill them by prayer if he so desired. John agreed that he would not seek their deaths, but clarified that he must then put their religion on trial. He then prayed that the demon that was beguiling the crowd would depart. After his prayer, the altar split in two, the food offerings that had been presented to Artemis fell on the floor, seven images were shattered, and half the temple fell down. As it did so, one of the pillars fell and crushed the priest of Artemis. Upon seeing this, the entire temple declared their monotheistic belief in the one true God and converted to

Christianity. John gave glory to God for the miraculous conversion and took the opportunity to continually jibe the lack of response from the false goddess, Artemis. His speech worked the crowd into a fury, and they went around destroying what was left of Artemis' temple.

After they had done this, the crowd pleaded with John to accompany him to his house. John acknowledged that he had planned to travel on to Smyrna to spread the gospel there, but that now he would remain in Ephesus until he had taught the rudiments of the faith to them and established a growing, sustainable church.

One of the members of the crowd that day had been a relative of the priest who perished when the temple collapsed. He was converted along with the rest of the crowd, but this did not change his love for his relative. As the crowd followed John back to his house, the man threw the priest of Artemis over his shoulder and carried him to the door of the house. He decided that presenting his relative's corpse to John immediately would be bad form, so he propped the priest up beside the door and entered to join the religious gathering. While inside, John prayed for the group, ate communion with them and laid hands on them to pray for them and commission them.

As John was ministering to the new believers in this way, the Holy Spirit revealed to him what had taken place with the priest of Artemis and his relative. John proclaimed this knowledge to the crowd and singled out the priest's relative from the crowd asking him if what he had said was true. The young man affirmed the truth of John's words and John reassured him that Jesus would demonstrate his power to them by raising his relative up from the dead. As he had done with Cleopatra, he taught the young man the resurrection formula. As soon as he had uttered it, the priest of Artemis rose from the dead. John then offered the gift of salvation through Jesus Christ to the priest of Artemis, who accepted it graciously. From that day forward, the priest joined the company of those who followed the Apostle John.

Chapter 5

John and the Patricidal Man

Then one day, according to the *Acts of John*, John had a dream that he should walk three miles outside the city gates. He believed fervently in the prophetic power of dreams and left early the next morning to take a walk with his close companions who were travelling with him. While they were walking the passed a farm where there was quite a bit of commotion. One of the field laborers was being warned by his father not to sleep with the wife of one of the other laborers, since the father had overheard the husband threatening his son. The son did not appreciate his father telling him how to behave and hauled off and kicked his father in the gut knocking the wind out of him. It must have been some blow, because John and his companions stood in the road watching as the father keeled over and died from it. While he was watching this scene, John prayed to the Lord, asking for confirmation that this incident was the reason he had been led out of the city on this day. They then saw the son remove his sickle from his belt where it rested during his heated argument with his father as he ran for shelter in his own home fearing imminent arrest for murder by the authorities.

John managed to intercept the young man on his was to his house and addressed him as a demon. The man then dropped the sickle from his hand and sobered up immediately from his demon-possessed haze. He then confessed remorsefully to John, not only to the deed he had just committed against his father, but to the further murders that he now planned to commit. He explained to John that when he saw that he had killed his father, he believed that all hope was lost and was just now on his way to kill the woman with whom he was having an affair along with her husband before he took his own life. He had thought that such an outcome would be better than to endure having his lover's husband witness him being given the death penalty.

At hearing the man's confession, John had compassion upon him and offered to raise his father from the dead if he would stop the affair that was causing so much grief for his family. The young man heartily agreed and brought John to where his father lay dead. At this point, a small crowd of travelers had gathered around the body brimming with curiosity regarding the recent events that had transpired there. After rebuking the young man in the presence of the crowd for killing his father, John recited the resurrection formula and the old man sat up quite perturbed. Looking at John he said, "Sir, I had finally been granted respite from this horrible and cruel life and from my sons constant insults and lack of concern for my well-being. Why on earth did you bring me back to life?" To this ungrateful response, John graciously replied that he was not raising him to his old life, but a new and better one.

The scene was too much for the son to bear and still wielding his sickle, of which no one had thought to relieve him, he cut off his penis. With blood spewing everywhere between his legs, he then took it in his hand and ran to his lover's house. He found her and her husband sitting at their kitchen table and in a grand gesture, placed his penis on the table and said, "It is because of you that I murdered my father and would just as easily have murdered the two of you along with myself. This [pointing to his penis] is the cause of all of this heartache. But God has been merciful to me." Having said his peace, he left.

But when the young man had been stitched up

and tried to relate his story to his fellow believers as a model of faith and dedication, John rebuked him. He clarified for the young man that his organs had not been the problem, but rather the thoughts that produced the behavior in the first place. This was the last significant event that took place while John was staying in Ephesus. The people of Smyrna again appealed to John to visit them and this time John and his companions obliged without delay.

John in Smyrna and Other Cities

The Acts of John describes that as soon as the people of Smyrna learned that John was in their city, they began bringing their sick to be healed by him. One such man was a civic leader in the community of Smyrna named Antipatros. He fathered two twin brothers, who had been plagued with epileptic convulsions since they were infants, which he believed to be the work of demons. The disease was a progressive one, and now that his sons had reached 34 years of age, Antipatros had begun to consider poisoning them so that they would no longer be forced to bear these violent fits. He offered John 10,000 gold pieces to heal his two sons. John politely refused clarifying that the payment that the Lord requires for healing is not monetary in nature, but rather, the souls of individuals. John then drove the demons out of the two boys healing them and subsequently baptized the entire family.

At this point, there is another large gap in the text. It would seem that the story went on to describe incidents of John's ministry to each of the seven cities who are the recipients of the letters to the seven churches in the book of Revelation. During one of these trips, Irenaeus appeals to a story he heard from Polycarp, that John the apostle went into a bathhouse one day to take a bath. While he was there, he learned that Cerinthus, a prominent heretic of the time, was also using the bathhouse at the same time. Upon hearing this, he leapt up from the bath and ran for the door without even stopping to collect his clothes. He explained to his companions that he wanted to leave the place immediately for fear that the place would collapse since Cerinthus was inside.

This gap is also where the tradition of John's exile to the island of Patmos would have been related if it belonged top this tradition. Eusebius records that when Nerva succeeded Domitian as Caesar, the Roman senate voted to remove Domitian's honors and to rescind any banishments from the region that he had imposed. This included the banishment of John, who was allowed to return to Ephesus (Eusebius, *Church History*, 3.20). But Clement of Alexandria indicates that John went first to check on the other churches of Asia he had established before returning to Ephesus. While he was checking on one church, he found a youth who impressed him in both physique and temperament. John asked the bishop of the place to raise the young boy in the faith. The bishop took an oath and agreed to raise the boy in the faith.

John Returns to Ephesus

John and his companions then set out on their return journey to Ephesus after a long absence, based on the *Acts of John*. Along the journey, the group stopped at an inn (more of a 'roach motel' as the following story will make clear). The room they checked into had only one bed that was not even made up. The men spread their cloaks over the bed and offered it to John while the rest of them slept on the floor. As John they there, he soon realized that the bed was infested with bugs. At about midnight, John had had enough of these bugs crawling all over him, so he cried out, "I command every one of you bugs to behave yourselves. You must leave your home tonight and remain quiet in one place so as not to disturb the servants of God." John's companions laughed at the scenario and John rolled over and went to sleep. When they woke up in the morning, they were astonished to find an enormous mass of bugs huddled in the corner of the room. John was the last to wake up, and when he did so, his companions explained that the bugs were in this corner when they awoke and had remained there the entire morning. John then sat up in bed and said, "You, bugs, since you have behaved yourselves as I commanded you, you may now return to your home." As soon as John climbed out of bed, the mass of bugs scurried across the floor and up the bed legs disappearing into the joints and mattress. John then noted that even these creatures are capable of being quiet and obedient to the voice of a man, but those who hear the voice of God continue to be disobedient.

The group then ventured on and arrived in Ephesus at last. They settled in and this time John stayed at the home of Andronicus. They caught up with old friends and heard news on the general state of the congregation. While they were staying there, a prominent citizen of Ephesus who was not part of the congregation, named Callimachus, fell in love with Andronicus' wife, Drusiana. When he confided in his friends his longings for this woman, they explained to him that he was mad. Not only was she a married woman, this was the same woman who had taken a vow of chastity that she refused to break even when her husband locked her in a sepulcher. He was mad if he thought that he could seduce her. He approached her a few times, but then gave up on his attempts before making a complete fool of himself. He then fell into a deep depression, pining for her in secret. For her part, Drusiana was quite upset that she had caused a man such spiritual agony and came down with a fever that made her bedridden. She asked that the Lord take her home so that she would no longer cause such suffering and she died from the fever shortly thereafter.

John then presided over her funeral and preached words of comfort on the occasion to the congregation and to her husband, Andronicus. While they were conducting the ceremony, Callimachus learned of her death and found Andronicus' steward, Fortunatus. Callimachus paid Fortunatus a whole lot of money to give him access to Drusiana's tomb. When Fortunatus asked him why he wanted access to her tomb, he explained that he wanted to have sex with her corpse. Fortunatus agreed accepting the bribe and helped Callimachus into her tomb. They found her lying on the stone slab in the tomb, and they both began to undress her corpse. She was down to her underwear and Callimachus took her outer garments out of the tomb and placed then neatly so that he could redress her when he had finished with his abominable deed. While Callimachus was outside the tomb, a snake appeared biting Forunatus and killing him instantly. When Callimachus reentered the tomb, he saw an angel covering Drusiana with his cloak. The snake then turned to Callimachus and choked the life out of him and then sat coiled upon his chest.

On the third day after the funeral proceedings, John and Andronicus prepared a communion meal to-go that they might eat at the tomb, as was the custom. They began looking for the keys to the tomb, but could not find them, as Fortunatus had taken them with him. John assured Andronicus no to worry that they would gain easy access to the tomb, and they set out. When they arrived at the tomb, they saw Drusiana's grave-clothes neatly folded outside, and the door was ajar. As they entered, an angel was standing beside the half-naked body of Drusiana, Andronicus' servant was lying dead in the corner along with some strange man from the community, Callimachus.

John surveyed the scene carefully, had a few opaque words with the angel, which foretold the resurrection of Callimachus and Drusiana, but was entirely perplexed by it. He admitted that he had no idea what had happened here and was somewhat alarmed that the Lord had not revealed the matter to him. But Andronicus, who recognized Callimachus as the man who had made advances toward his wife and had heard further rumors that he had vowed to sleep with her corpse if she would not have him while living, reconstructed the scenario for John. He then invited John to raise Callimachus from the dead, as the angel had foretold, so that he could confirm the reconstruction with his own confession. John then turned to the snake still perched upon Callimachus and ordered it to depart, which it did. When John uttered the resurrection formula, Callimachus rose from the dead, but sat in shock and silence for an hour.

When he finally spoke, he confessed his sins and confirmed the reconstruction that Andronicus had provided. He also confirmed that he did not succeed with his plans because he was interrupted by the angel and the snake. Moved by his resurrection and now repentant, Callimachus believed and converted to Christianity. With Callimachus now a believer, Andronicus believed that the reason his wife had asked to die was no longer relevant and asked John to raise Drusiana from the dead a second time. John consented, speaking the resurrection formula and raising Drusiana from the dead. Now accustomed to the whole dying and rising again thing, she was more flummoxed by why she was in the tomb in her underwear. Her husband explained the situation to her as delicately as he could while he handed her back her outer garments. She took it in stride and praised God for the miracle.

Drusiana then took issue with the fact that their house servant, Fortunatus still lie dead in the tomb and asked John to raise him as well, forgiving him for betraying her. Callimachus objected to her request arguing that because the angel only spoke to him about the resurrection of Drusiana and himself, that it must not be God's will to raise Fortunatus. But John came up with a clever workaround that would appease the concerns of Drusiana and Callimachus. He entrusted the task of raising Fortunatus to Drusiana. Remembering the resurrection formula she had previously used with her husband, Drusiana gladly recited it over the body of her servant, Fortunatus. Confirming the concerns raised by Callimachus, Fortunatus was anything but grateful to Drusiana for raising him from the dead. He quickly took stock of the situation making sure those standing around knew full well that he would rather have stayed dead and then ran away from the tomb. When John heard the ungrateful response of

Callimachus, he called after him a series of curses that would prevent him from any possibility of future salvation. The group then proceeded to have the communion meal that they had initially planned to eat there at the tomb.

They then returned to the house of Andronicus where John received a revelation that Fortunatus would soon die of a snakebite. He sent one of his followers to verify his vision and the follower returned shortly thereafter with news of Fortunatus' death.

John and the Prodigal Ward

According to Clement of Alexandria, some business then came up that called John back to the city where he had left the young boy in the care of the bishop. He travelled to the city and after he completed his business, approached the bishop asking for the return on his deposit. The bishop became confused thinking that John was asking for some money that he had never received. Perceiving the confusion of his friend, John clarified that he was referring to the boy he had left in the bishop's care. The bishop began to cry stating that the boy was dead. When John enquired as the circumstances of his death, the bishop elaborated that the boy was dead to God.

The boy had fallen in with a rough crowd with whom he committed robbery. The boy then moved on to even more heinous crimes and became the leader of the gang.

When John heard what had become of the boy, he asked for a horse and for a guide to show him the way. Supplied with both, he set off in search of the boy. As they approached their destination, they were accosted by a group of bandits. John was not alarmed, but asked the infamous question, "Take me to your leader." As soon as the boy saw John, he was filled with shame over what his life had become, and he began to run away. John, in his turn, ran after the boy calling to him that he had no reason to fear this unarmed and old man that he was. He pled with the boy to repent and offered to atone for the boy's sins with his own death if need be. The boy was overcome and threw down his weapons and repented of his sins. John stayed with the boy for quite some time and did not return to Ephesus until the boy was restored to fellowship with the church (Clement of Alexandria, *The Rich Man who Finds Salvation* 42:1-15).

The Death of John

Returning to the narrative of the *Acts of John*, some time later John held a large communion service with the congregation blessing each of them individually. At the conclusion of the service, he took three members of the congregation with him along with a set of shovels and baskets. He led them to a graveyard outside the city and stopped beside the grave of another member of the congregation and asked his companions to begin digging. When they had dug a sufficient size trench for his needs, he walked into the trench taking off his outer garments and lying them down in it so that he was left standing in his underwear. He then extended his hands toward heaven and prayed a long prayer rehearsing the highlights of his life and thanking God for it. When he concluded his lengthy prayer, he lay down in the trench, which was now unmistakably a grave, and died. Several early Christian writers corroborate this tradition that John died of old age in the city of Ephesus. Eusebius, Irenaeus and Polycarp all agree in this tradition (Bernard, 1908, 53).

Chapter 6

A Biographical Sketch of the Writer of the Fourth Gospel

Whereas John, the son of Zebedee, was a Galilean by all accounts, the author of the fourth Gospel was clearly not from Galilee. In contrast to the Synoptic Gospels, the author of the Fourth Gospel is hardly interested in Galilee at all, allowing Jesus only three trips to the region during his ministry. When he does focus on Galilee, he makes a fairly egregious error when it comes to the relative distances between cities in the region. In the Fourth Gospel only, Jesus is located in Cana when the father of the sick boy travels from Capernaum to see him. According to the story, the father meets Jesus at about one in the afternoon, where he relates his son's dire condition (John 4:47, 52-53). Jesus considers it for a moment and then gives a flippant remark about faith (John 4:48). The father reiterates his case pleading for Jesus' help and Jesus finally relents and instructs the man to return home reassuring him that his son will live (John 4:49-50). The man then complies with Jesus' instruction and returns home (John 4:50). From the context, there is no reason to think that the man would have dilly-dallied in any way on the return trip to check on his sick son. But only the author of the Fourth Gospel adds the detail that it was the following day when the father met up with his servants on the road to his house.

This information that the evangelist has added does not seem to track with the facts of the local geography. Capernaum was only 42 kilometers from Cana and given an average walking speed of 5 and a quarter kilometers per hour, the father would have arrived in Capernaum around nine in the evening (or the fifteenth hour of the day, but certainly the same day) if he were walking at a standard leisurely pace (Parker, 1962, 37). But the mitigating factors in this case were that his son was gravely ill and that Capernaum (205m below sea level) was more than 500 meters downhill from Cana (343m above sea level). Given those two mitigating factors, it is likely that, from the story's perspective, the father would be travelling at an above average walking speed on his return journey. This would put the father home only an hour or so after sundown and, possibly earlier, if he were travelling at a brisker pace. The simplest explanation for this faux pas is that the evangelist did not have first hand knowledge of Galilee.

In addition, the author of the Fourth Gospel is downright ignorant about James, John's brother and Salome, who was likely their mother. Neither James nor Salome is mentioned at all in the entire gospel presentation. It is possible, as Brown argues, that the evangelist was concerned with anonymity, and this is why he refers enigmatically to himself and avoids mentioning his mother or brother by name for this same concern for anonymity (Brown, 1966, XCVII-XCVIII).

The author of the Fourth Gospel knew Greek well and wrote in impeccable Greek. It was certainly not as well written as other Classical Greek writings, but it does not correspond to the statement made in Acts that Peter and John were illiterate. Some scholars have noted that in the context, illiterate may refer more to ignorant of the Jewish and Mosaic Law as opposed to simply uneducated. But even if this were the meaning, the author of the Fourth Gospel had a thorough knowledge of Mosaic Law.

In addition, the author of the Fourth Gospel was quite contemplative, whereas John, the son of

Zebedee, is described as bold and a man of action (Acts 4:13). Not only was he bold, but he was quite interested in exorcism. Not only does the Fourth Gospel spend limited time relating the deeds of Jesus as opposed to his words, it does even record one of the exorcisms of Jesus.

Each of these internal characteristics of the Fourth Gospel stand at variance with the knowledge provided elsewhere about the son of Zebedee. Whoever, the 'Beloved Disciple' was that stands behind the Fourth Gospel, it is clear that it was not John, the son of Zebedee.

The Epistles of John

Unlike the letters of Paul, the letters attributed to John make no direct claim to their authorship. The letter known as First John makes absolutely no reference to its author. The other two letters, known as Second and Third John, reference their author only as 'the elder.' According to Eusebius, the early church universally accepted the first letter as authoritative. The second two letters remained in dispute in his time. Papias is the first early church writer to make reference to two Johns. He mentions John the evangelist and apostle, and then later he mentions John the presbyter (also translated 'elder').

Recent scholarship argues that the author of First John cannot be identified with the author of the Fourth Gospel. Additionally, the author of Second and Third John most likely stems from a different hand than either of these two previous books. A few common themes emerge, especially between the gospel and the first epistle, but the differences are far more striking and deep-seated.

The Book of Revelation

In his Church History, Eusebius records that John was still alive during the reign of Domitian (81-96 CE). He notes that John was sentenced to the island of Patmos during Domitian's reign, because of his preaching. It was during this time that he wrote the Book of Revelation.

The Book of Revelation does indeed to claim to be written by a figure named John who was exiled to the island of Patmos for preaching the Word of God (Rev. 1:9). As with the epistles, the language and themes of the Apocalypse are totally divergent from those covered in the Fourth Gospel and those of the three Johannine epistles.

The authorship of this book was a source of great dispute in the early church, and it was one of the last to make it into the canon. Some recent scholars have argued that because of the apocalyptic content of the book that it fits much better with the thought of John the Baptist than with John, the son of Zebedee. Most modern scholars, however, are more content to chalk this book along with the epistles and the Fourth Gospel up to four or five different anonymous authors.

Chapter 7

James Travels to India

According to the Ethiopic *Contendings of the Apostles*, James, the son of Zebedee, received the lot to travel to India to preach the gospel. As he did with all of the evangelistic missions of the twelve apostles, Peter accompanied James in his initial departure to India. While the two were travelling, the risen Christ appeared to them on the road. He assured them that one hour of rest in the kingdom of heaven would be sufficient to cover all of the pain and suffering they had experienced in this world. Jesus then further reassured them by presenting all of the righteous who had died from Adam until the present. He then offered a word of encouragement to James, telling him to preach the name of Jesus to the world and that thereby he would gain a great reward.

Peter and James, now resolved and reassured, continued together on their journey. On the highway, they encountered a blind man begging for bread. This man entreated the apostles to restore his sight. James then deferred to Peter in the matter. At which point Peter informed James that he would be the one by whose hands the healing would flow. James was eager for the opportunity and asked for Peter's blessing, which Peter gladly gave straightaway.

James then turned to the blind man and proposed a hypothetical to him. Suppose I were to open your eyes, he said, in that case would you believe in Jesus Christ. The blind man affirmed that, in such a case, he would believe wholeheartedly. James then uttered a healing formula before the blind man and his eyes opened easily, and he began to see. Some of those who witnessed the miracle accused the two apostles of sorcery, which was the only source of healing they had previously seen, and took their case to the city elders.

The city leaders then asked the apostles to declare their intentions. Once Peter identified them to the authorities, the authorities responded by ordering that the guards place ropes around their necks so that they might be dragged through the city and defamed as sorcerers. When the guards tried to place the ropes around the necks of the apostles, their hands dried up and withered and their legs locked up. The authorities became upset with the guards for their insolence and berated them accordingly. When the guards explained what had happened, the authorities cited that as further proof of the apostles' sorcery.

The apostles rebutted this accusation explaining

that their power was not a result of being sorcerers, but of being servants of God. The guards found hope in the apostles' claim and appealed to them on this basis to heal affected limbs. At that point, both Peter and James turned to the guards and pronounced a healing formula upon them. This resulted not only in the physical healing of these guards, but also in a declaration of faith in Jesus Christ from these guards and from several onlookers. The narrator emphasizes that these were declarations of a monotheistic faith, which would have been unheard of on the Indian subcontinent.

Now one of the authorities, who had harassed Peter and James, was named Theophilus. This Theophilus had a son whose feet were withered preventing him from walking. After witnessing the healing power of these two apostles, he decided it would be worthwhile to bring his son before them in the hopes that they might heal him. If indeed they proved successful, he would in turn confess faith in their deity. Theophilus asked one of his servants to bring his son to these apostles. The servant went immediately to the family home and notified Theophilus' wife that some healers were in town and that he needed to take her son back to Theophilus, where these healers were. The servant returned with the son shortly thereafter.

At first Peter and James prayed together that God would be glorified in the ensuing healing miracle. Peter then ceded the floor to James, who uttered the healing formula. At once, the man rose to his feet and quickly began walking. The crowd who was assembled responded by declaring their faith in the God of the apostles. Moreover, the father of the lame boy, overcome with emotion, invited the apostles to his home for a meal. Wanting to share his newfound joy with his wife, he immediately sent his son home to his wife. She had been anxiously awaiting the return of her son and became overjoyed when she saw him walking down their street. She, as well, declared her faith in the God of the apostles.

James and Peter had accepted Theophilus' gracious invitation to supper. But as a leader in the Indian community, Theophilus had previously worshipped the gods of the Indian pantheon and had many of their idols throughout his home. As soon as the apostles entered his home, the idols fell from their shelves breaking in pieces. Rather than upsetting the couple, this miraculous event served to strengthen their faith in their newfound God. The apostles then sat down to a nice home-cooked meal with their newfound friends. Theophilus offered many gifts to Peter and James for them to distribute to the poor. The apostles kindly refused his offer asking instead that he deliver these goods directly to the poor himself. They also baptized him and his entire family providing them with a copy of the Law and the Prophets. They established a church in the region before Peter returned to accompany other apostles on their missionary journeys.

The Death of James

According to the Book of Acts, James, the son of Zebedee was killed by the sword by King Herod Antipas. This was the same king who was responsible for the death of John the Baptist. Since he died in 39 CE and Jesus' death is dated around 33 CE, this James had a limited time to influence the early church. This relatively short lifespan compared with that of his brother, who lived to a ripe old age according to the most reliable sources, helps to explain the relative obscurity that surrounds this James in the tradition. Although he was one of the inner circle of three and would have otherwise played a central role in the growth of the church, his life was cut short before he could have a significant impact on the church.

Bibliography

Bernard, J. H. "The Traditions as to the Death of John the Son of Zebedee." *The Irish Church Quarterly* 1 (1908) 51-66.

Brown, Raymond E. *The Gospel According to John*. 2 Vols. Garden City, NY, 1966.

Budge, E.A. Wallis. *The Contendings of the Apostles*. 2 Vols. New York, 1901.

Culpepper, R. Alan. *John, the Son of Zebedee: The Life of a Legend*. Columbia, SC,

1994.

Derrett, J. Duncan M. "James and John as Co-Rescuers from Peril (Lk. V 10)." *Novum Testamentum* 22 (1980) 299-303.

Metzger, Bruce. *The Textual Commentary on the Greek New Testament*. Stuttgart, 1975.

Schäferdiek, Knut. "The Acts of John." Pp. 152-209 in Wilhelm Schneemelcher (ed.) *New Testament Apocrypha: Vol. II. Writings Related to the Apostles Apocalypses and Related Subjects*. Louisville, KY, 2003.

Made in the USA
San Bernardino, CA
02 March 2014